Published by Creative Education
123 South Broad Street, Mankato, Minnesota 56001
Creative Education is an imprint of The Creative Company

Designed by Stephanie Blumenthal
Production Design by Mae Stewart

Photographs by Bonnie Sue Photography, Grant Heilman Photography,
Root Resources, Tom Stack and Associates, Marilyn "Angel" Wynn

Library of Congress Cataloging-in-Publication Data

Wrobel, Scott
Ranching / by Scott Wrobel
p. cm. — (Let's Investigate)
Includes glossary and index
Summary: describes what is involved in raising beef cattle and how ranchers
feed, care for, transport, and sell their livestock.
ISBN 0-88682-976-3
1. Ranching—West (U.S.)—Juvenile literature. 2. Cattle—West (U.S.)—Juvenile
literature. [1. Ranching. 2. Cattle.] I. Title. II. Series: Let's Investigate
(Mankato, Minn.)
SF197.5.W76   1999
636.2'0883'0978—dc21   98-7857

First edition

2 4 6 8 9 7 5 3 1

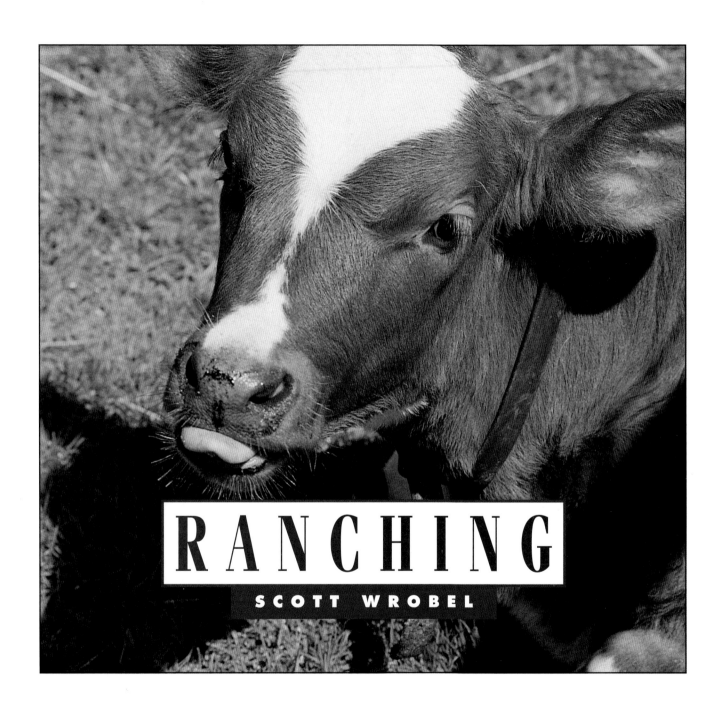

RANCHING

SCOTT WROBEL

Creative C Education

RANCH

More than 200,000 cowboys of the American Old West were black slaves who had been freed after the Civil War.

Above, llamas are raised on ranches for wool Right, cattle need large areas of grazing land

Of all the creatures in the world, cattle are one of the most important to humans. Images of cattle have been found painted on walls where prehistoric cave dwellers once lived, as well as inside ancient Egyptian tombs. Cattle were once traded for services, property, and other livestock, and were even included as terms in marriage agreements. Today, cattle ranching is important to the various industries that provide meat and milk for food and leather for clothing and other products.

RANCH

STRAY

A cow, bull, or calf that has strayed away from its herd is called a maverick.

RANCH

SHOWS

In the United States, cattle shows are popular. Cattle are judged on muscle tone, udder quality, and other factors, and the winning owners receive money and ribbons. The purpose of these shows is to improve livestock breeds.

Many ranchers still use horses to gather their herds on the range

RANCHING HISTORY

Cattle are a member of the Bovine family of animals, domesticated long ago into two common groups we know today as cows (females) and steers or bulls (males). These two main types of cattle are raised as **livestock.** Beef cattle are grown on large and small ranches for meat, while dairy cattle are raised in **herds** for the milk they produce. The major breeds of beef cattle include Longhorn, Shorthorn, Hereford, and Red and Black Angus.

Farmers who raise beef cattle are commonly called ranchers. Most ranching in North America takes place on large areas of land west of the Mississippi River. On some of these vast lands where cattle herds number in the thousands, the cattle outnumber people.

RANCH
TRAIN

It wasn't until 1891 that processed beef could be transported by train in refrigerated boxcars.

Ranching is a family tradition in many U.S. western states

RANCH

LASSO

What ranchers today call a **halter** used to restrain cattle, was called a lasso back in the days of the Old West ranchers.

8

Cattle operations east of the Mississippi are called cow farms or livestock farms because they use less **grazing** land and rely more on **feedlots.** In western North America, some cattle ranches are so large that the ranchers must brand their animals in order to keep track of any that might wander away. Horse ranches often follow this same practice.

Above, branding irons
Right, branding a calf

RANCH

HORN

Unlike antelope and deer, which have antlers that are shed each year, cattle have hollow horns that never shed.

RANCH

FAMILY

The term ranchers and farmers use to describe the act of a cow giving birth to a calf is "calving."

A branded calf with an ear tag

This is done with a red-hot iron pushed into the cow's skin. The brand is usually a series of numbers or letters that identify the owner of the cow or bull. On many large ranches, one might see cowboys on horseback rounding up the cattle. This is an old tradition dating back to the days of long cattle drives across many miles from the ranch to the market.

Cowboys faced many dangers, including attacks by Native Americans wanting to keep the cattle off their land and raids from thieves called cattle rustlers. Flash floods and thunder storms could cause stampedes, with the animals running perilously out of control. Today, most large herds are fenced in, or corralled, and are monitored by ranchers using pickup trucks, four wheelers, and even helicopters.

Center, many cattle ranches are in the mountainous states of the western U.S. Above, calves are sometimes bottle-fed

RANCH
RELATIVE

From the moment they are born until they are eventually processed for their meat, beef cattle require a lot of care. Animal doctors, called veterinarians, are often hired to help ranchers care for cattle. A cow or calf may need to be vaccinated, or given medication to prevent or cure disease. Ranchers may also need to spray the animals with **pesticides** to get rid of pesky fleas or mosquitoes, dehorn or brand them, test their blood, trim their hooves, or simply wash them.

Domestic cattle are related to the wild American buffalo, as well as the yak and the Indian and African buffalos.

11

RANCH
MONEY

Because cattle are easily startled and not very intelligent in the way that dogs and cats are thought to be, they must be restrained in **cattle chutes** when they receive medical care. Ranches have many types of cattle chutes, each with its own purpose. For example, the squeeze chute keeps the head from moving. Other kinds of chutes are the tilt table, foot-trimming chute, grooming chute, and working chute.

Cattle in a confinement area awaiting medical check-ups and treatment

Barbed wire fencing
was invented in
1876, after most of
the wild grazing land
was sectioned off
and turned into pri-
vate ranch land.

13

C attle kept in large herds can be prone to disease and **parasites.** They need to be vaccinated on a regular basis, either by a needle injection or by a liquid solution that is placed on their tongues—a process called drenching. **Antibiotics** are often mixed in cattle feed. Pesticides, which do not injure the cattle, are often sprayed on the animal's skin to keep biting insects away.

Ranchers lasso each animal to separate it from the herd when giving medical treatment

RANCH
STARS

The constellation of stars called Taurus, often referred to as the bull, gets its name from an early species of bovine called Bos taurus.

Center, longhorn bull Below, sheep have traditionally been an enemy of cattle ranchers, as sheep can permanently destroy cattle grazing land by overfeeding on the grasses

14

Dehorning is a process that removes an animal's horns in order to prevent injury by other cattle when sharing close quarters. Not all breeds of cattle are dehorned. Longhorns, for example, have magnificent horns that are often left to grow long.

Male cattle are often sterilized so they can no longer reproduce. Bulls that have good qualities are kept for breeding.

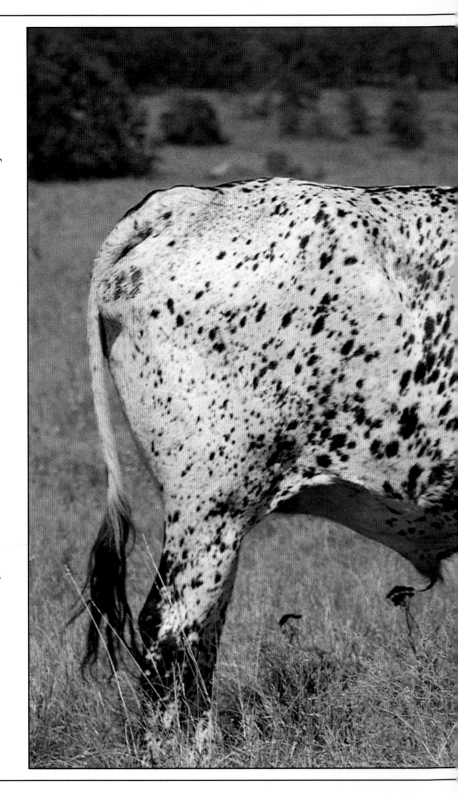

RANCH
HISTORY

The Hereford breed of cattle takes its name from the place of its origin, Herefordshire, England, where they were originally bred to pull plows rather than provide meat.

16

Cow in an open shed Opposite, fresh hay is made available to cattle throughout the day

Many ranch operations include unheated buildings that provide cattle with shelter from cold winter weather. When the animals huddle together inside the shelter, their combined body heat helps to keep them warm. A common shelter in the Midwest is a large, rectangular building called an open shed. The sides and roof are usually made of metal to protect the animals from wind, rain, and snow. The front side is open, allowing the cattle to enter and exit freely.

RANCH
IMPORT

Two popular cattle breeds, the Black Angus and the Red Angus, were originally bred in northern Scotland and later imported to the U.S.

Feed trough

Shelters also provide a place to feed cattle. Unlike buffalo, which are wild animals native to the Great Plains of North America, domestic cattle are not very strong diggers. They cannot penetrate snow and ice to get the grasses and grains that grow on the prairie.

For this reason, ranchers build feeding troughs inside the shelters or along the sides of the **corral.** The troughs are stocked with plenty of primary food sources.

This includes oats, grains such as cracked corn, and hay or alfalfa. Additional protein and vitamins are added to the feed. Most shelters also have mineral boxes filled with salt and other **minerals** that add nutrition to the diet of cattle.

All this healthy food supplemented with vitamins and minerals helps the cattle grow big and meaty.

RANCH
PACKER

The first U.S. meat packers were the early colonists, who packed meat in salt to preserve it; Native Americans prepared buffalo meat in dried jerky strips.

Left, cattle feed includes alfalfa pellets (top) and a mixture of cracked corn and various grasses (bottom) Below, a market-weight Hereford steer

RANCH
BURGER

About 24 percent of a slaughtered beef animal is used to make hamburger; 14 percent is used to make cold cuts, such as bologna.

Above, winter feeding Center, cattle are often kept in corrals during the winter

In the summer, cattle that are left to graze in fields or on the **prairie** are often provided with sun shades in various places across the grazing land. These structures are simply metal roofs over wooden posts. Cattle can gather under them, out of the sun's heat. Water is also vital to ranching. In areas without ponds or streams, wells must be dug and pumps used to bring water from deep underground. Water is kept in watering troughs, long, rectangular wooden frames lined with cement or metal that hold large amounts of water.

During the winter, cattle are rounded up and brought in from the range. The water troughs used in winter are refilled often to prevent freezing. Circulating watering troughs may also be used. These are similar to standard watering troughs except that an electric pump is used to move the water around in the trough, keeping it from freezing. Some pumps are powered by windmills.

RANCH
MIXTURE

Longhorn cattle meat was considered too lean, so breeders crossed Longhorns with Herefords to create a meatier animal.

RANCH

The United States is the world leader in beef production, which also makes it the largest and most successful agriculture-based industry in the nation.

Yearling calf

RANCH

SALES

When cattle are sold alive, each animal is weighed and given a "grade and yield" value, which is based on approximately 60 percent of the animal's total weight.

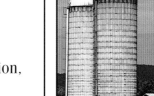

Silos can hold grain or silage for cattle and other animals to eat

CATTLE BREEDING

To insure successful breeding, or reproduction, veterinarians often assist ranchers during breeding season. Usually one bull is mated with an entire herd of both cows and heifers—females that have not yet given birth. Ranches may house bulls in pastures separate from the cows until mating time. This controls breeding and reduces the risk of injury to the cows. On many ranches, cows are kept separated from the bulls and are bred artificially.

24

ewborn cattle are called calves. A calf can walk almost immediately. It will remain close to its mother and feed on her milk for six to eight months. At 12 months of age, the young cattle, called yearlings, weigh about 650 pounds (295 kg). They are fully weaned by this time and eat cattle feed.

For the next six months to one year, they will fatten up for market. The average weight of beef cattle ready to be sold is 1,100 pounds (500 kg).

Right, cows stay close to their young for months, protecting them Opposite, horses left to roam on ranches must be rounded up to be trained for work or to be sold

RANCH
CONTROL

RANCH
NEIGHBOR

Horse ranching is an important industry; unlike cattle, which are eaten, most ranch-raised horses are used as working animals or sold as race horses.

Loading cattle onto a truck for transport to the processing facility

MEAT PRODUCTION

Cattle must be transported from the ranch or the feedlot to the market in order to be sold. To move the cattle, they are first moved to a holding pen, a large fenced-in area where many cattle can be kept together. Attached to the holding pen is a loading chute. This is a narrow fenced ramp that leads from the holding pen into a livestock trailer or truck.

Stockyards are large areas where livestock are temporarily penned and fed until they are sold at auction. It is common for cattle to wear ear tags almost from the moment they are born. A metal wire is stapled into the ear. Attached to the wire is a tag with a code that might tell the type of animal, its gender, and the name of its owner. Combined with branding, this makes identification of the animal on the range and after it is sold quite easy.

A controversial issue in South America and Africa is the practice of destroying rain forest land to make way for beef cattle grazing pastures.

Left, ear-tagged steer Above, barbed wire is usually all that is needed to keep cattle in their proper territory

RANCH

Ranching is hard work, and so is meat processing. Meat-packing jobs are considered "high risk," with the injury rate of this occupation very high.

28

Below, clean bedding is vital to cattle health Center, Brahman cattle are kept on southern ranches, where the weather can be very hot

Tagging is important, since thousands of cattle may be penned together in a stockyard before being transported to the processing facility.

Most of these facilities are owned by food companies. These companies must abide by various animal protection laws that require the slaughter of livestock to be quick and painless.

Once that is done, the beef is usually cut into large portions and sold to butcher shops or grocery stores. There, butchers divide the meat into smaller portions such as steaks, roasts, and ribs; some of the meat is also ground into hamburger.

Black Angus is a breed of cattle known for its delicious steaks. Many restaurants and butcher shops sell steaks that are specifically labeled "Black Angus."

RANCH
PARTS

Roughly 15 percent of a beef cow or steer is considered by-product; this is the hide, fat, and bones of the animal used to make such non-edible products as glue, cosmetics, and even pet food.

29

Black Angus cattle

RANCH
HISTORY

Suffering the loss of buffalo herds, Native Americans in the late 1800s began to raise beef cattle herds.

RANCH
HEALTH

Beef is a healthy food source when prepared properly and not over-consumed; a three-ounce (85 g) serving of lean beef has about 200 calories and less than 10 grams of fat.

Right, blue ribbon winner Opposite, bringing cattle in from the range is called a cattle drive

CATTLE ARE VALUABLE

Cattle supply half of the world's meat, most of the world's milk, and more than half of the world's leather. The United States is the world leader in beef imports, meaning that it buys more beef from other countries than any other nation. Much of this beef comes from South America, where cattle ranching operations are enormous. The U.S. is also a major exporter of beef—other countries buy tons of U.S. beef each year.

Cattle breeding has become an important **genetic** science.

GEORGIA NATIONAL STOCK SHOW 1994

JUNIOR HEIFER

FIRST PLACE

Leather from cattle is made into numerous things, from clothing to furniture coverings. In the nation of India, however, cattle are not processed for food or leather. Rather, they are worshipped as an important symbol of the Hindu religion. Cows wander freely throughout busy city streets and country villages. Many breeds of cattle are used as working animals in countries around the world, pulling plows and carrying packs. Oxen, a type of cattle, are especially valued in farming communities of Asian and African countries. From Canada to Argentina, and Russia to India, people of virtually every nation on earth appreciate the value of cattle.

The Brahman was developed in the country of India to provide milk and to work; it is a favorite in the southern U.S. because it is well-adapted to hot, humid regions.

Glossary

Antibiotics are medicines that fight infection and disease.

Cattle chutes are tightly enclosed, fenced spaces used to hold individual cows fairly motionless.

A **corral** is used to enclose large numbers of cattle or other ranch animals, such as horses.

Large plots of land, not as large as ranches, where cattle are raised and fed for slaughter are called **feedlots.**

Among other things, **genetic** science and research involves the study and development of breeding animals to achieve the most desirable traits in the offspring.

Grazing is when animals feed on growing plants or grass.

A rope or leather strap with a noose used for restraining cattle is called a **halter.**

Herds are groups of animals that stay together or are kept and raised together.

Livestock is the word used to describe cattle, sheep, goats, and other useful animals raised on a farm or ranch.

Minerals, such as salt, are specific substances necessary for proper nutrition in animals and people.

Small insects, animals, or plants that live on or inside another plant or animal to take nutrients from it are called **parasites.** Many parasites cause disease or even death.

Pesticides are chemicals—prepared substances in liquid or powder form—that are used to kill unwanted insects.

A **prairie** is a large, flat area of land that is mostly treeless and contains a wide variety of plants and grasses.

Index